For William

Composer's World

Ludwig van Beethoven
by Wendy Thompson

VIKING

Introduction

England is famous for its great literature, France and Italy for painting and sculpture, but the prize for music must go to Germany and Austria. Haydn, Mozart, and Beethoven, three of the greatest composers the world has ever known, were all born within less than fifty years of each other, and all worked in and around the same place – Vienna. But their lives and careers were all very different, and reflected the tremendous changes that were taking place in society as the eighteenth century gave way to the nineteenth.

Haydn, the oldest and longest lived, spent much of his life quite happily under the "patronage" system of the Old Regime. His employer, Prince Esterházy, treated him as a valued servant, and allowed him a degree of freedom, but he still had to produce music to order when the Prince wanted it. Haydn was very lucky to have such a tolerant employer, who gave him a secure job with a good salary.

Mozart, twenty-four years younger, was brought up in the same system, working for the Archbishop of Salzburg. But he rebelled against such restrictions, and made a brave attempt to win independence and freedom by working as a freelance performer and composer in Vienna. But in the 1780s, Austrian society still maintained a strict pecking order: the aristocrats held the purse strings, while ordinary people struggled to make a living as best they could. In spite of his brilliant talents, Mozart found his life governed by people who thought him an arrogant little upstart. His

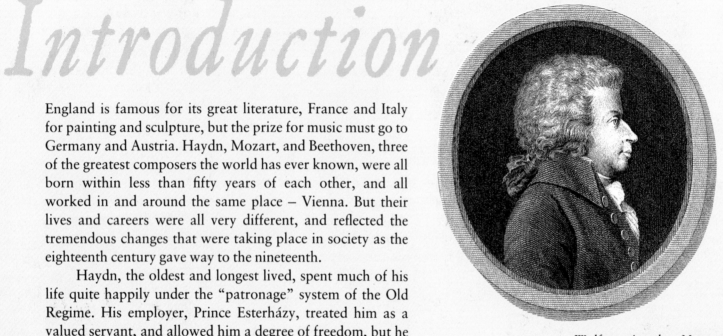

Wolfgang Amadeus Mozart (1756–1791)

career was eventually destroyed by other musicians' jealousy, and by his own refusal to play the part of the humble, cringing courtier.

But by the time Beethoven was a young man, in the 1790s, times were changing fast. In the year he was born, 1770, a fateful marriage took place, between the fifteen-year-old Dauphin Louis, heir to the throne of France, and Marie Antoinette, the thirteen-year-old daughter of the Empress of Austria. This important alliance between the two most powerful dynasties in Europe was celebrated with bonfires, fireworks, banquets, and general rejoicing. Only twenty-three years later, the whole of Europe watched

The execution of Marie Antoinette

people living in extravagant luxury in sumptuous palaces, unaware and unconcerned about their subjects' problems. But like many violent social upheavals, the French Revolution quickly ran out of control. In the two years of Terror that followed, many thousands of ordinary people – as well as the hated aristocrats – lost their heads. When other nations, such as Austria, protested, France simply declared war on them.

Out of this chaos, a young French General called Napoleon Bonaparte saw a chance to create a better social order, with fairer laws and more equal opportunities. But soon, ambition got the better of him. Over the next twenty years the whole of Europe was plunged into the whirlpool of war, as Napoleon, now the Emperor of the French, tried to take over the world. Not until Wellington finally defeated him at the Battle of Waterloo in 1815 could the citizens of other countries breathe freely again.

horrified, but unable to help, as first the King, and then the Queen of France went to the guillotine. The age of Revolution had arrived. Spurred on by the example of the Americans, who in 1776 had thrown their British masters out and declared themselves a free and independent nation, the French middle and working classes finally decided that they had had enough of paying through the nose to support a few

The leaders of the Allied Armies meet in Leipzig after the Battle of the Nations in 1813

The French were not the only people who wanted Liberty, Equality, and Fraternity – noble aims which had produced such violence in France. In countries where no bloody revolution took place against the ruling classes, even the most conservative people had begun to realize that the new century must see a basic change in attitudes. When Beethoven was three, a book was published which had almost as powerful – though much less explosive – an effect on people's lives as Tom Paine's famous *Declaration of the Rights of Man* (the manifesto of the French Revolution). This book was *The Sorrows of Young Werther*, by the great German writer Johann Wolfgang von Goethe. The story, which is partly based on Goethe's own experiences, tells how a young and sensitive man falls in love with a married woman, and eventually commits suicide because of his unhappy passion. Nowadays, our more cynical society might find this a bit extreme, but in the late 1700s, its effect was tremendous. Young men dressed in "Werther" clothes, young ladies wept over it, suicide became fashionable, there were operas, plays, poems about *Werther*. This was the book which really set off the "Romantic" age, in which the feelings of the individual person were considered more important than his or her social status. As we shall see, it had echoes in Beethoven's own unhappy personal life. *Werther* was Goethe's first major novel, and he went on to dominate German literature for over half a century. Beethoven worshipped him. In 1823 he wrote him a letter, speaking of the "admiration, love and esteem" which he had felt for the writer, even as a youth.

When Beethoven was born, the world had changed very little for the past hundred years. Living conditions were quite primitive, and the horse was still the fastest means of transport. By the time he died, fifty-six years later, social, political, and industrial revolutions had completely changed

A scene from Goethe's Werther: *the last interview of Werther and Charlotte*

people's lives. Incompetent kings were losing their thrones to new republics, gas lamps were replacing candles for lighting, electricity had been discovered, steam locomotives had been running for over ten years, and the first steamships had crossed the Atlantic. While Haydn and Mozart showed little interest in politics, being content to do as well as they could inside the social structure they knew, Beethoven was very conscious of his own rights as a human being. He lived through a revolutionary age, and his music reflects the violence, passion, struggle, and upheaval of those times, as well as the quest for personal and spiritual fulfillment.

1770–1792

1 Bonn

Beethoven, like Mozart, was born into a musical family, and their early lives followed somewhat similar paths. Beethoven's grandfather was Kapellmeister (music director) to the Archbishop-Elector of Cologne, whose court was based in the town of Bonn, on the Rhine (now the capital of West Germany). Although it was small, dirty, and provincial, Bonn was even then an important place: the Archbishop-Elector was one of the most powerful of the 300 or so rulers of states which made up the territory called Germany; and his court was rather splendid. The Archbishop, together with other aristocrats in the town, kept his own orchestra, and the city was constantly visited by well-known musicians.

Beethoven's father Johann also worked for the Archbishop-Elector as a singer and a rather poor instrumentalist. In 1767 he married a young widow, and settled down in a house on the Rheingasse (now No. 7). There seven children were born to the couple, but like Leopold Mozart and his wife, they lost several. Ludwig, the eldest survivor, was born on December 15 or 16, 1770 (the exact date isn't certain), and his two younger brothers, Caspar Carl and Nikolaus Johann, arrived four and six years later.

The house where Beethoven was born
(No. 934 in the Rheingasse)

5

Beethoven's father wanted his eldest son to follow in young Mozart's footsteps as a child prodigy pianist (Mozart's name was then on everyone's lips), so he taught him piano and violin when he was very young, keeping him at it for hours at a time. Not surprisingly, little Ludwig was often exhausted and in tears. He gave his first public concert at seven, and was sent to the local primary school, where he stayed for three years. That was his only real schooling, which accounts for his bad spelling and punctuation, and the fact that in later life he couldn't do even the simplest sums. Ludwig didn't mix well with his schoolfellows. "How dirty you look," said one of them. "You should try to be tidier." "What difference does it make?" replied Ludwig. "When I am a gentleman, nobody will notice."

When he was not at school, Ludwig was having lessons from the old court organist and other local musicians. In 1781 he began to study composition and keyboard with Christian Gottlob Neefe, who had recently arrived to work for the Elector. Neefe saw that the boy had great promise, and by 1782 he allowed the eleven-year-old to deputize for

*Christian Gottlob Neefe (1748–1798),
Beethoven's first important teacher*

C. G. NEEFE.

him as court organist – quite a responsibility! The next year, Neefe persuaded a Mannheim publisher to print a little set of variations for keyboard by Beethoven, and had him made accompanist and keyboard player to the court orchestra. When Ludwig was twelve, another of his compositions was published – this time a set of three piano sonatas, dedicated to the Elector.

In 1784 the old Elector died, and the Empress's youngest and favorite son, Maximilian Franz, succeeded him. A keen music-lover, Maximilian promoted Beethoven to second organist, with a proper salary. At the same time,

One of Beethoven's earliest piano sonatas, in F minor

Allegro assai

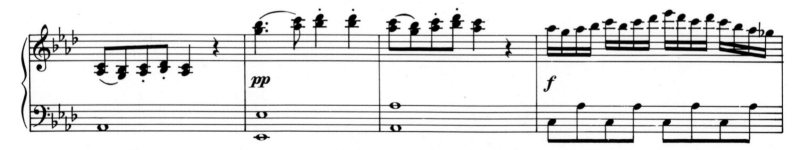

The Breuning family's house in Bonn

incurable) disease. His father, by now deeply in debt, was often to be found in the local police cells, blind drunk. At the age of eighteen, Beethoven made himself head of the family and asked the Elector to allow him half his father's salary as well as his own, to support his younger brothers. The Elector, a kindly man, agreed.

Apart from these family troubles, life was getting better for Ludwig. He had made friends with Count Waldstein, an influential person and a great supporter of music. Waldstein encouraged Beethoven's musical talents, gave him money, and made it possible for him to study the classics and attend philosophy lectures at Bonn University. In the winter of 1790, the great Joseph Haydn visited Bonn on his way to London. It is not known if Beethoven was introduced to him then, but he may well have met him when Haydn was on the way back; shortly afterward Waldstein persuaded the Elector to let Beethoven go to Vienna again, this time to study with Haydn.

In 1792 war was declared between France and Austria. Late that year, with the advancing French army hard on his heels, Beethoven set off, leaving his two young brothers and his dying father behind. In his pocket was a note from Count Waldstein which ended:

Through your unfailing efforts, receive Mozart's spirit from Haydn's hands. Your true friend, Waldstein.

Ludwig made an important social contact – with the local von Breuning family, who engaged him as a piano teacher for their daughter Eleonore. The von Breunings were intelligent and cultured people, who let Beethoven have the run of their beautiful home and large library. There he was able to read the best and most up-to-date German literature. The contrast between this and his own home, where his mother was seriously ill and his father was taking to drink, couldn't have been more marked.

When Beethoven was fourteen, he was forced to give lessons to support his parents. However, he still found time to take a few violin lessons, and he went on composing. In 1787 he was sent to Vienna to study with Mozart. "Keep your eyes on him," said Mozart to his friends. "One day he'll give the world something to talk about."

But his lessons were cut short almost immediately by a family tragedy. On July 17, 1787 his mother died in agony, of tuberculosis. Beethoven, who adored her, was devastated, and was afraid that he might catch the dreaded (and then

Count Waldstein (1762–1823)

9

2   Early Years in Vienna

Vienna in the late eighteenth century was the most important and powerful city in Europe. It was not very big – the city center, clustered around St. Stephen's Cathedral, took up less than a square mile. But its dominant position, right in the middle of the continent, on the banks of the Danube – Europe's longest and most navigable waterway – gave it commanding political and economic advantages. To the west, outside the city walls, was the magnificent Schönbrunn Palace, from where, during the summer, the Hapsburg Imperial Family ruled their far-flung empire. Inside the city, rich and poor lived crowded together, the rich occupying the best and most luxurious apartments of the town houses, with poorer families in the attics and basements. Although the upper classes spent money wildly – throwing magnificent dinners and masked balls, attending the opera, taking carriage rides in the Prater, gambling, and organizing hunting

A view of Vienna

parties — it was all taken for granted by ordinary people. This meant that the tidal wave of hostility that had engulfed the French royal family in the splendid isolation of Versailles passed Vienna by. So life went on much as before; but it was an artificial way of life, already out of date.

The twenty-two-year-old Beethoven set about trying to make contacts and create a good impression. Out of his tiny income he bought himself a new outfit, took some dancing lessons and rented a small attic room. From there he soon moved into a room in a mansion on the Alserstrasse belonging to Prince Lichnowsky, who had been one of Mozart's patrons. Beethoven's lessons with Haydn, however, were not a great success. He didn't feel he was learning anything and soon went (secretly) to another teacher for lessons in music theory and composition. Eventually, Haydn left for London, without taking his brilliant pupil with him, and Beethoven felt free to go openly for lessons with two well-known Viennese musicians, Albrechtsberger, and Salieri (Mozart's old rival).

Beethoven soon began to make a name as a pianist; he had an incredible talent for improvisation (composing music at the keyboard). "He is greatly admired for the fantastic

Prince Carl Lichnowsky (1756–1814)

velocity of his playing and astounds everybody by the way he can master the greatest difficulties with incredible ease," reported a local magazine. Fashionable Vienna accepted this small, dark, belligerent young man, and in 1793 the famous Viennese firm of Artaria published his set of variations on a theme from Mozart's *Figaro* for violin and piano. More importantly (since he was practically penniless), he began to attract some influential patrons, who took an interest in him – Baron Gottfried von Swieten (Mozart's former patron), and his own landlord, Prince Lichnowsky, who was to be one of his chief friends and supporters. Within a couple of years, Beethoven had moved from one little room to a whole suite of·elegant rooms in the Prince's mansion. It was ironic that Mozart, who was brought up in the proper way of speaking to his superiors, and who always took care with his clothes and personal appearance, should have been rejected by a society that apparently welcomed the uncouth Beethoven. "He was small and plain, with an ugly, red, pockmarked face. His dark hair hung shaggily round his face. Moreover, he spoke in a strong dialect, and behaved rather boorishly," recalled a society hostess.

Joseph Haydn (1732–1809)

*The Burgtheater in Vienna, where many of
Beethoven's concerts were held*

12

On March 29, 1795, Beethoven gave his first public concert at the Burgtheater (where Mozart's *Figaro* had been performed). He played his own Piano Concerto in B flat (now know as No.2), and his playing was praised for its "passionate strength." The concert was a great success, and Beethoven quickly followed it up with another, at which he played Mozart's great D minor Piano Concerto, and improvised brilliantly. Then Artaria published three of his trios for piano, violin and cello, dedicated to Prince Lichnowsky. Haydn advised his pupil not to publish the third, even though Beethoven thought it was the best. When all three, and especially the third, proved very popular, Beethoven unjustly accused Haydn of trying to damage his career; and when he published his next compositions, a set of three piano sonatas, with a dedication to his teacher, he deliberately left out the customary "pupil of Haydn" on the title page. But by December 1795 the two seemed to be on friendly terms again: Beethoven played his new Piano Concerto (in C major, known as No.1) in a concert together with three symphonies by Haydn.

By 1796 Beethoven's star was rising fast. He had been asked to write some music for one of Vienna's most important society balls, and he was able to set himself up in his own apartment on the fashionable Kreuzgasse, where he had his own horse and servant. His two brothers were finally off his hands – both had come to Vienna and found jobs. Now, Beethoven decided it was time to go on a concert tour (something Mozart had done from the age of six onward). His first trip took him to Prague, Dresden, Leipzig, and Berlin, where he played for the King of Prussia and was rewarded with a gold snuffbox full of money – "fit for an ambassador," according to Beethoven.

Over the next three years Beethoven continued giving concerts and publishing music. In 1796–7 he followed the Op.5 set of cello sonatas with some piano sonatas, and a set of keyboard variations on a dance from a popular Viennese ballet. The husband of the Countess to whom Beethoven dedicated the variations gave him a horse, which he rode a few times, and then forgot even to feed! The Quintet, Op.16, for piano and wind, and one of a set of very unusual violin sonatas (which a reviewer found "bizarre and painful") were performed for the first time; the Emperor and his family attended a concert of Beethoven's music at the Court Theatre; and Beethoven took part in an improvisation competition with the pianist Joseph Wölffl. "Beethoven has great facility on the piano," reported Ignaz Pleyel, another talented pianist, "but his playing isn't polished. He is a fiery player, but he pounds a bit too much. His improvisation is not cold, like Wölffl's, but he sometimes plays anything that comes into his head, and does quite astonishing things."

And just as the eighteenth century gave way to the nineteenth, Beethoven published a magnificent new piano sonata in C minor, the "Pathétique" – a truly Romantic work which opened up visions of a new age.

Slow movement from the "Pathétique" Sonata (original key Ab major)

The title-page of the "Pathétique" Sonata, Op. 13

3 Crisis

Up to now, Beethoven had seen himself mainly as a concert pianist, and his compositions as a profitable sideline. But on April 2, 1800, at his first "benefit" concert in Vienna (a concert from which he took all the proceeds himself), a piano concerto (either No.1 or No.2), and two major new works were played – the popular Septet, Op.20, dedicated to the Empress of Austria – and the Symphony No.1. Just as Mozart is most famous for his operas and his piano concertos, Beethoven's most important works are his symphonies.

The audience didn't really know what to make of the symphony. One reviewer described it a work of "great charm, novelty and many ideas" – which was a polite way of saying that he was baffled. "There is something revolutionary about that music," remarked the Emperor Francis I, acidly. Unlike Mozart, who, trained in the Italian tradition, was able to weave his pieces around beautiful melodies, Beethoven found it very difficult to write a good tune. Instead he used a few "motifs" or germ cells of musical material – not very interesting in themselves – to build up huge structures held together by a powerful sense of rhythm. Though Beethoven took as his starting point the Classical symphony in four movements developed by Haydn and Mozart, the sheer amount of material he packed into it was already beginning to stretch the framework to its limits. While the third movement of the symphony was still the usual minuet and trio, in Beethoven's hands it was no longer a courtly dance, but a fast, dramatic piece full of violent contrasts. By the time the next symphony came along, Beethoven had decided to replace the minuet with a new type

Louis van Beethoven

Beethoven at the age of 30

of fast movement called a "scherzo" (which literally means "joke") – and many of the scherzo movements show off his sense of humor.

"Who is this Beethoven?" people were beginning to ask. But just as they began to realize that a startling new talent had burst upon them, Beethoven, then still only thirty, reached an appalling crisis in his personal life. He was beginning to go deaf. He had been having trouble with his hearing for four or five years, but it took him a long time to accept the fact, and he tried to keep it a secret for as long as possible. He wrote to one of his friends that he was feeling utterly wretched, and felt he could not live a normal social life. What would people think? After all, a deaf musician was about as much use as a blind painter. "In my profession this is a terrible condition. Sometimes, if someone speaks in a low voice, I can barely understand, and if anyone shouts, it is unbearable. Heaven knows what will become of me." And

Countess Giulietta Guicciardi (1784–1856)

what made matters worse, Beethoven badly wanted to find himself a wife and settle down. He spent much of his adult life falling in love with various ladies, some of them already married, nearly all from a higher social class. One of these was a Hungarian countess, Josephine von Brunsvik, whom Beethoven had taught the piano a few years earlier. Poor Josephine was married off at twenty to a dubious character old enough to be her father, who ran a waxwork museum in Vienna. After her husband died a few years later, Beethoven hoped that she would think about marrying him, but Josephine had had enough of marriage. Another young girl who caught his fancy was the sixteen-year-old Countess Giulietta Guicciardi, but she was quite out of his class. Although Beethoven dedicated the famous "Moonlight" Sonata to her, as proof of his love, she married another composer – who just happened to be a Count.

Josephine von Brunsvik (1779–1821)

Opening of the "Moonlight" Sonata *(original key C♯ minor)*

Adagio sostenuto

pp

con ped.

In spite of his affliction, Beethoven went on composing. He finished a set of string quartets and a string quintet, and in March 1801 his first work for the stage, a ballet called *Prometheus*, was performed at the Burgtheater. The next year he decided to spend the spring and the summer at the village of Heiligenstadt, just outside Vienna, hoping that the country air would improve his health and his hearing. Soon he and his sketchbooks became a familiar sight, as he wandered in the fields, gazed at the breathtaking views across the Danube to the Carpathian mountains, took sulphur baths on doctor's orders – and finished another symphony, three violin sonatas, two piano sonatas, and several shorter piano pieces. But his hearing didn't improve, and by October, he was reduced to such misery that he sat

Beethoven in 1801

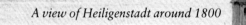

A view of Heiligenstadt around 1800

down and wrote a long letter to his brothers. This letter was found after his death, and is known as the "Heiligenstadt Testament." Beethoven wrote frankly of his hopeless position, forced to accept that he would never be cured. "For me there can be no pleasure in human society, no intelligent conversation, no mutual confidences, I must live like an outcast." The humiliating experience of being with someone who remarked on the sound of a distant flute or a shepherd's song, and hearing nothing, wrote Beethoven, "brought me to despair, and I was on the point of putting an end to my life . . . It seemed impossible to leave the world before I had brought forth all I was destined to do . . . Patience must now be my guide . . . Oh Providence, grant me just one day of pure joy . . . for so long this has been denied me." But having reached the depths of despair, Beethoven returned to Vienna determined to fight and overcome his disability. A new phase in his life was about to begin.

The last page of the letter known as the "Heiligenstadt Testament"

4 A Heroic Struggle

Apart from his personal problems, Beethoven was doing rather well. His concerts were popular, his playing was getting better all the time, Prince Lichnowsky had given him a regular income, and now he was asked to write an opera for one of Vienna's principal theatres, the Theater an der Wien. He was also allowed to use the theatre for private concerts, and on April 5, 1803 his new oratorio, *Christ on the Mount of Olives*, was performed there. Eighteenth-century audiences would have scoffed at our modern one-and-a-half or two-hour concerts: this programme was massive. Apart from the oratorio, which lasted nearly an hour, it included both the First and Second symphonies, some vocal pieces, and a new piano concerto (No.3 in C minor). The rehearsal began at eight o'clock in the morning, and went on (with a short break for lunch) until just before the concert, which started at six in the evening. Luckily for Beethoven there was no Musicians' Union then! Beethoven had no time to write out the piano part of the concerto, and played it from memory. Not surprisingly he made many mistakes, and although the concert made him quite a lot of money (1800 florins, or about $6000 now) the new oratorio was a disappointment. The audience found it long and boring, and it has never been one of his most popular pieces.

Beethoven in 1804, painted by J. W. Mähler

The Theater an der Wien around 1815

A month or so later, Beethoven gave another first performance, this time accompanying the half-black violinist George Bridgetower in the great violin sonata known as the "Kreutzer," after the famous French violinist Rodolphe Kreutzer, to whom Beethoven dedicated the piece. (He was apparently going to dedicate it to Bridgetower, but the two men quarrelled over a girl, and Beethoven changed his mind at the last minute.)

He was shortly to change his mind over a dedication again. He spent the summer of 1803 in Oberdöbling, near Vienna, working on a new symphony. This was to be called the "Bonaparte," in honor of the man whom Beethoven saw as the savior of France. But in May 1804 Napoleon decided to crown himself Emperor, and in a fit of rage and disillu-

SINFONIA EROICA

The title-page of the "Eroica" Symphony

sionment Beethoven seized the title page and tore it in two. The symphony was published in 1806 with a dedication to Prince Lobkowitz, to which Beethoven added meaningfully: "to celebrate the memory of a great man."

This symphony, now known as the "Eroica," is a piece of truly heroic proportions. By far the longest symphony written by anyone up to then – it is nearly twice as long as some of Mozart's – it also needs a bigger orchestra, with three horns instead of two. The second movement is a powerful and tragic Funeral March – which perhaps symbolized the death of Europe's hopes for a better future. Once again when the symphony was first performed, people didn't know what to make of it. One reviewer remarked on its "startling and beautiful passages," but nearly everyone agreed that it was much too long – Beethoven just didn't know when to stop. In fact one member of the audience was heard to mutter, "I'll pay another kreutzer if only the wretched piece would finish!"

George Bridgetower (1779–1860), the virtuoso violinist

Funeral March from the "Eroica" Symphony

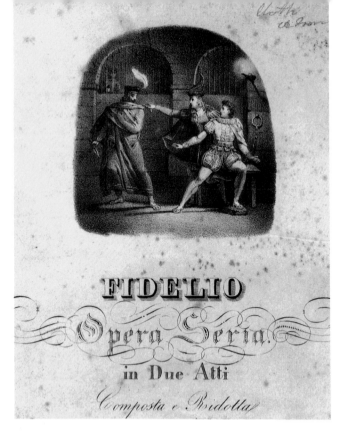

The title-page of a score of Fidelio

Beethoven kept up this heroic mood for some time to come, in the Triple Concerto for piano, violin and cello, two massive piano sonatas (the "Waldstein" and the "Appassionata") and his only opera, *Fidelio*. The plot of *Fidelio* was taken from a French play set during the Revolution, which tells of a wife's heroic efforts to save her husband's life. The story was very popular, and several composers made operas out of it. For political reasons (the French army was closing in on Vienna), Beethoven moved the scene from Revolutionary France to sixteenth-century Spain. Florestan, a freedom fighter, has been put in prison and his life is in danger. His wife Leonore decides to stage a rescue attempt. Disguised as a boy called Fidelio (faithful), she gets herself taken on at the prison as assistant to the jailor. Pizarro, the evil governor of the prison, decides to kill Florestan, but is stopped by Leonore. Just at that moment, a trumpet call heralds the arrival of the Minister of State to inspect the prison. Pizarro is arrested, the prisoners are released, and Florestan is reunited with his wife – who clearly represents Beethoven's ideal woman, brave and loyal. (Beethoven once said that he couldn't understand how Mozart could write such frivolous operas as *Così fan tutte*, about two fickle girls.)

But it wasn't only on the stage that courage was needed in 1805. By the beginning of November the citizens of Vienna were starting to panic. Napoleon's army had reached Salzburg, and the aristocracy were frantically loading up their possessions and shipping them eastwards out of harm's way. On November 13, the French marched into Vienna. "For a few weeks a most unusual silence reigned," wrote an observer. "The court, the courtiers and most of the great landowners had left; instead of the usual rattle of coaches through the streets, one rarely heard even a cart go by. The streets were mostly full of French officers and many people stayed at home. The theatres were also quite empty at first . . ." A week later, *Fidelio* had its first performance to a virtually empty house – consisting mostly of French officers – and it was taken off after three performances. Shortly afterwards, nearly 30,000 Austrian troops were killed at the Battle of Austerlitz. Napoleon, whom Beethoven now loathed – "I made a mistake with that Bastard," he said – forced the Austrian Emperor to sign a peace treaty, and Vienna slowly began to return to normal.

Like many of Beethoven's works, *Fidelio* was felt to be far too long. Beethoven agreed to revise and shorten it, and it was put on again in the spring of 1806. But then he had a major fight with the theater's owner, demanded his score back, and marched out in a temper. Vienna did not hear the opera again for another eight years.

Count Razumovsky's palace in Vienna

5 Fame

Beethoven was determined to prove that deafness was no handicap to him. Even after finishing *Fidelio* he didn't stop for a rest, but ploughed straight on with another group of important compositions. The first of these was a group of three unusual string quartets – very long and difficult – dedicated to the Russian Ambassador to Vienna, Count Andreas Razumovsky. As usual, when the quartets were first played, the audience thought Beethoven was playing a joke on them with this "crazy music." But within two years, people came to accept them and they were published in 1808.

Beethoven spent part of the summer of 1806 at Prince Lichnowsky's castle at Grätz, where he finished his next symphony – No. 4 in B flat, for which he was paid 500 florins ($1680 now). This symphony is a smaller, more appealing work than the "Eroica," and its lively style pays an indirect compliment to Beethoven's old teacher, Haydn. By the end of the year he had also finished his wonderful Violin Concerto, which was first performed just before Christmas in Vienna by the violinist Franz Clement. As was the custom of the time, Clement played the first movement in the first half of the concert, and the other two in the second half, with some showy "trick" pieces in between. Not surprisingly, the audience couldn't make much of Beethoven's piece – now acknowledged as one of the greatest violin concertos of all time.

The next March he put on two more concerts of his own works at Prince Lobkowitz's palace. The programs included his four symphonies, a new piano concerto (the enchanting No. 4 in G major), and a new overture, to the popular play *Coriolan*. This piece, about the life and tragic

A page from Beethoven's manuscript of the first "Razumovsky" Quartet, Op. 59 No. 1

death of the Roman hero Coriolanus, was an instant hit. Shortly afterwards, Beethoven signed a contract with a publisher based in London to have his works published there. He was also asked by Haydn's old employer, Prince Nikolaus Esterházy, to write a mass. Beethoven himself conducted the first performance of the Mass in C at a church in Eisenstadt near the Prince's palace on September 13, 1807. The experience was not a happy one. Beethoven, like Mozart, resented being humiliated by his social superiors, and always insisted on being treated as an equal. But old habits die hard, and many aristocrats found it difficult to stop treating musicians as if they were servants. At Eisenstadt, Beethoven was not given a room in the palace, but was lodged with other employees in a damp, squalid room. After the concert, the Prince jokingly said to him, "What's all this then, my dear Beethoven?" while the court music director sniggered. "Beethoven's Mass is unbearably ridiculous and horrible, and I don't think it can ever be properly performed," wrote Esterházy privately to a friend. Beethoven was furious. Although religious music was then rather out of fashion, he knew his mass was outstandingly good, and soon afterwards it was translated from Latin to German, so that more people could understand it.

Just before Christmas 1808, the Viennese were once more bowled over by another Beethoven marathon concert, this time containing two new symphonies – No. 5 in C minor and No. 6 in F (the "Pastoral"). As if that were not enough, Beethoven also played his fourth Piano Concerto, his new Choral Fantasia for piano, chorus, and orchestra, and conducted other bits and pieces, including sections from the Mass in C. Four hours of music altogether, in a bitterly cold theater, with a tired, bad-tempered and badly rehearsed orchestra, and difficult singers – it wasn't surprising that the audience's reaction was mixed! Now, any concert which

includes Beethoven's Fifth (his most popular symphony) is sure to be a sell-out. "It carries the listener away irresistibly into the wondrous spirit world of the infinite," wrote the great German writer E.T.A. Hoffmann. "It is conceived with genius, executed with great thoughtfulness, and expresses the romantic spirit in music in the highest degree."

The Fifth Symphony is indeed quite revolutionary, both in design (the same musical material is used to link the movements together) and scoring (with added piccolo and trombones, which weren't normally used in orchestral works of that time). It opens in the "tragic" key of C minor, but the last movement blazes out triumphantly in the "radiant" key of C major. Many people believe that this progression from darkness to light represents Beethoven's personal struggle against defeat and despair. The famous four-note motif of the opening – "fate knocking on the door" as one critic described it – is coincidentally Morse Code for the letter "V", and it was used by the Allied Forces in World War II as a secret symbol for "victory!"

The Esterházy castle at Eisenstadt

Opening of the Fifth Symphony

The Theater an der Wien

The "Pastoral" Symphony is completely different. In it Beethoven tried to put into musical language scenes from life in the country – a quiet day out in the fields, the babble of a stream, a village festival (interrupted by a sudden thunderstorm), and to end, a shepherd's song describing "happy and thankful feelings after the storm." It was this piece which really opened up the age of musical Romanticism, in which composers depicted paintings, landscapes and stories through their music. "You ask me where my ideas come from," wrote Beethoven to a friend. "I can't tell you exactly . . . I could grab them in my hands, out in the open air, in the woods, out walking, late at night, early in the morning, brought on by moods which the poet can put into words and I into sounds which whirl round me until I can get them down as notes on paper."

That incredible concert marked the end of Beethoven's career as a concert pianist – he found he couldn't get on with orchestras, who were refusing to play for such a demanding and handicapped soloist. He even considered leaving Vienna for a well-paid job at the court of Kassel, but three of his aristocratic friends – the Archduke Rudolph (the youngest son of the Emperor, and Beethoven's friend and pupil), Prince Lobkowitz and Prince Ferdinand Kinsky – got together to find a way of keeping Beethoven in Vienna. They drew up a contract guaranteeing him a good annual income of 4000 florins ($13,440 now) plus other benefits such as the use of the Theater an der Wien for his own concerts once a year. Beethoven, his financial problems temporarily solved, started work immediately on a new piano concerto, No. 5 (the "Emperor").

1806–1809

Opening of the "Emperor" Piano Concerto

Beethoven's three patrons:
Prince Lobkowitz (1772–1816)

But by May 1809 Vienna was in turmoil again. Napoleon's armies had once more invaded, and by May 11, the city was under heavy artillery bombardment. While shells burst around his house on the city's ramparts, Beethoven sat in a cellar with a pillow over his head to shut out the noise. The next day, the city surrendered. A French nobleman who visited Beethoven in his lodgings found "a very ugly man, visibly in a bad temper." He was appalled by the squalor in which the world's greatest composer was living: in two small, dirty, untidy rooms, covered in dust and mold, an unemptied chamber pot under the bed, and the remains of several nights' suppers left lying around on chairs.

Beethoven hated the Occupation. He could not get out to the countryside, and all residents of Vienna were forced to pay crippling taxes to the French. By the end of the year things were a little better. The Emperor's eighteen-year-old daughter, Princess Marie-Louise, had been hastily married off to Napoleon (who had just divorced his first wife, Josephine), and France had signed a "peace" treaty with

Prince Ferdinand Kinsky
(1781–1812)

Archduke Rudolph von Hapsburg
(1788–1831)

Napoleon Bonaparte (1769–1821)

Austria. Beethoven managed to finish his Fifth Piano Concerto (dedicated to the Archduke Rudolph), the "Harp" String Quartet, and several new piano sonatas, including the "Farewell" (*Das Lebewohl*), begun when the Archduke and his family left occupied Vienna, and completed when they returned from exile in January 1810. The middle movement is called "Absence."

By that time Beethoven had had many more works published, including the new symphonies, another cello sonata, and a set of piano trios. His three faithful patrons confidently expected great things of their tame composer.

The bombardment of Vienna by Napoleon's troops

6 The Immortal Beloved

But for the time being, his patrons were to be disappointed. Beethoven was tired, ill, and worried about money: and during the next eight years, his mind was often on things other than music. In October 1809 he was asked to write some music for Goethe's play *Egmont*, about a Flemish general who died defending his country against invaders. The subject seemed highly appropriate, and appealed to Beethoven. "I wrote it purely out of love for the poet," he said, and he refused to accept any money for it. Shortly after its first performance, on June 15, 1810, Beethoven went through another crisis – he fell in love with the beautiful Therese Malfatti, the niece of his doctor, for whom he wrote the popular piano piece "Für Elise." He proposed to Therese, but she turned him down. He was now almost forty, and still hadn't found his ideal woman.

Piano Bagatelle "Für Elise"

In the summer of 1811, Beethoven's doctor advised him to take the waters at the Bohemian spa of Teplitz. There he wrote incidental music to two more plays, *King Stephen* and *The Ruins of Athens*. On returning to Vienna in the autumn he began work on two new symphonies, No. 7 in A major, and No. 8 in F. Once again these pieces are very different in character — one is a joyous celebration in dance-like

A view of Teplitz in the early 19th century

Turkish March from "The Ruins of Athens"

rhythms, the other a smaller, more formal piece in the classical mould. While working on the Eighth Symphony, Beethoven once more went to Teplitz, where he met Goethe. The great poet felt sorry for the unfortunate composer, whose deafness made him difficult and unsociable. "I have never seen a more energetic or intense artist," wrote Goethe. "I understand very well how strange he must seem to the world." On July 6, 1812, Beethoven began to write a letter, which he never sent and which was found after his death in a secret drawer of his bureau. It is an unfinished, passionate declaration of love to an unknown woman, whom Beethoven calls the "Immortal Beloved," and speaks longingly of a time "when we can live together." Who was the Immortal Beloved? No one has ever answered the question: one of the possibilities seems to be Antonie Brentano, an aristocratic Viennese lady married to a Frankfurt businessman, who lived in Vienna between 1809 and 1812. If she was the object of Beethoven's love, nothing ever came of it, since she and her husband went back to Frankfurt in the autumn of 1812, and Beethoven never saw her again. Many years later he dedicated one of his greatest piano works, the "Diabelli Variations," to her.

Beethoven had other problems in 1812 – the year that Napoleon's fortunes finally turned with his disastrous invasion of Russia. After leaving Teplitz, Beethoven visited Linz, where he had a major family fight with his brother Johann (Beethoven disapproved of Johann's choice of wife). But his own failure to find someone to love him made him deeply depressed, and although he tried hard to devote himself to "things of the mind" it was not easy, and he began to think of suicide once more. To add to his depression, everyday life in Vienna was very hard: the war had caused the value of

1810–1815

Beethoven meets Goethe at Teplitz

35

A poster advertising a performance in London of the Battle Symphony, *1816*

money to fall dramatically, and Beethoven's allowance was already greatly reduced. One of his patrons, Prince Kinsky, had been killed in a riding accident, while Prince Lobkowitz had himself fallen upon hard times and had temporarily withdrawn his part of Beethoven's income. Only the Archduke Rudolph remained a faithful supporter. To make matters worse, Beethoven was also having trouble with his other brother, Caspar Carl, whose wife he also hated, and who was seriously ill. In April 1813 Caspar Carl signed a document making Beethoven the guardian of his only son, six-year-old Karl. Young Karl was to cause his uncle many problems in the last years of his life.

On June 21, 1813 Napoleon's army was defeated by Wellington at the Battle of Vittoria in Spain, and to celebrate the occasion, Beethoven wrote the "Battle" Symphony, for

The French army marches into Vittoria

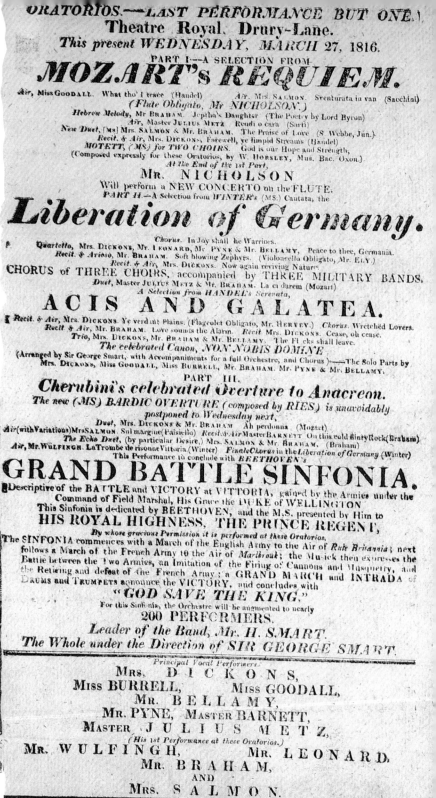

Statesmen at the Congress of Vienna

*Beethoven in 1814,
by Höfel*

an early kind of synthesizer called the "panharmonicon," which could imitate the sound of an orchestra. Later Beethoven re-scored the piece – which is not one of his best – for a real orchestra. It was first performed at Vienna University on December 8, 1813, with the new Seventh Symphony. The audience was ecstatic, and the concert raised over 4000 florins for wounded Austrian soldiers. The Eighth Symphony, played shortly afterwards at a concert in February, was not quite so popular as the Seventh. In April 1814, Beethoven appeared once more on the platform as a pianist, in his "Archduke" Trio, written in 1811 for his patron. The concert was a disaster. The piano was badly out of tune, but Beethoven couldn't hear it; in loud passages he pounded the keys "till the strings jangled," and in soft ones he played so quietly that the other performers couldn't hear him. Nevertheless, his reputation continued to rise in Vienna, and he was asked to revise his opera *Fidelio* for a new production.

To everyone's delight, it was finally a great success. It is now considered one of the finest operas ever written.

In the summer of 1814 it was announced that Vienna would host a great Congress, at which Europe's heads of State would sort out the mess left by the Napoleonic Wars. For nine months, the city became a huge pleasure garden, offering an endless round of balls, concerts, exhibitions, shooting parties, fireworks, and other diversions. Over 100,000 visitors poured in, from royalty, ministers, diplomats and their households, to artists, writers, actors, dancers and a train of less reputable characters, all hoping to cash in on the action. Beethoven's triumph was complete when he was presented to the Empress of Russia, to whom he dedicated a piano polonaise. Vienna wanted the world to know that this was her most celebrated composer.

7 The Last Years

The Napoleonic nightmare was over. The man who had caused so much misery in Europe had been exiled to his lonely island, but life for most Viennese citizens was not much better in peacetime. Fear of invasion was replaced by other restrictions under Count Metternich's government – censorship of letters, compulsory registration, special permits for travellers, and the dreaded secret police with their network of spies. Beethoven, who took a keen interest in politics, found the new regime distasteful and unsuited to creative work, and the next five years were relatively barren. Apart from two cello sonatas, Op 102, the song cycle *An die ferne Geliebte* (To the distant beloved – the last work he dedicated to Prince Lobkowitz, who died in 1816), and the Piano Sonata in A, Op 101, he wrote nothing between 1815 and 1817 but "occasional" pieces such as a march for the Vienna Artillery and a few Scottish folk-song settings. Despite earning good fees from his published pieces, Beethoven continued to worry about money, particularly since he had taken on a new responsibility.

His brother Caspar Carl had died in November 1815, and Beethoven found himself guardian of his nine-year-old nephew, Karl, jointly with Karl's mother Johanna. Beethoven hated Johanna, whom he regarded as a woman of

An anonymous portrait of Beethoven in middle age

loose morals, so he went to court to win sole custody of his nephew (who was clearly a substitute for the son he never had). In January 1816 Beethoven managed to persuade the court that Johanna was unfit to bring up Karl, and he was appointed the boy's legal guardian. But Johanna continued to challenge the decision, and it was not until 1820 that Beethoven finally won his case.

By 1818 Beethoven was stone-deaf. He abandoned the ear-trumpet he had used for several years and began a series of "conversation books" in which his visitors wrote down what they wanted to say. He also found a new publisher, who found him difficult to deal with. In those days, composers' works were not protected by copyright law. In order to gain what he felt was rightfully his, Beethoven resorted to tricking his publisher, pretending that old works were new ones, while offering the same pieces to other publishers.

In the autumn of 1817 Beethoven was invited to London by the Philharmonic Society, who asked him to write two new symphonies, but he never accepted the invitation. Instead he began a new piano sonata, bigger than any he had yet written. This was the "Hammerklavier," dedicated to the Archduke Rudolph. Rudolph was about to be honored by the Church – he was to be made Archbishop of Olmütz in Czechoslovakia – and Beethoven promised his patron a new High Mass to celebrate the event. While working on the Mass, Beethoven broke off to begin a set of piano variations on a theme by the Viennese composer and publisher Anton Diabelli, who had asked a number of well-known composers each to write a single variation on his tune, intending to publish them as a collection. But Beethoven went ahead and completed his own set of thirty-three variations. It was the last piece he ever had published for the piano – the instrument he loved so much.

A drawing of Beethoven, based on the famous portrait by Ferdinand Schimon

A page from Beethoven's manuscript of the Missa solemnis

His work on the Diabelli Variations, together with time-consuming lawsuits over Karl's custody, and a spell of illness, meant that he didn't complete the new Mass – the *Missa solemnis* – in time for the Archduke's enthronement. In fact, his finest sacred work, written "from the heart to the heart," was not finished until the autumn of 1822, and was never heard complete in Vienna in Beethoven's lifetime.

Beethoven at work on the Missa solemnis, *painted by J. C. Stieler*

The same year, having finished three more piano sonatas (Opp 109–111), Beethoven started work on another massive enterprise – the Ninth Symphony. For many years he had wanted to set to music the famous "Ode to Joy" by the German poet Schiller, and since 1815 he had been toying with the idea of a "choral" symphony with voices. Unlike Mozart, who composed music practically as he breathed, composition didn't come easily to Beethoven, and many ideas were jotted down in his sketchbooks, tried out and rejected, before a piece finally took shape. "I carry my ideas about with me for a long time before I write them down," he told a friend. "I change a great deal, eliminate much, and begin again, until I am satisfied with the result. Then the working-out begins in my head, and since I know what I want, I hear and see the work in my mind in its entirety." We know from the sketchbooks that Beethoven was thinking of ending the new symphony with "Turkish music and a vocal chorus," in keeping with the current fashion in Vienna for all things "Turkish."

On May 24, 1824 the Ninth Symphony was first performed at the Kärntnerthor Theater in a concert which also included an overture and bits of the *Missa solemnis*. Beethoven didn't conduct but stood on the platform to direct the performance. At the end, the audience went wild – but Beethoven couldn't hear the cheers. One of the soloists gently turned him towards the auditorium, to show him the people "throwing their hats in the air and waving their handkerchiefs!" The Ninth Symphony is a work regarded by later composers as a peak of achievement; indeed several – such as Dvořák, Bruckner, Mahler, Sibelius, and Vaughan Williams – found themselves so awed by its significance that they too were unable to finish more than nine symphonies. Beethoven's "Ninth" has the usual four movements, with the powerful scherzo coming second, but the last movement is

The Kärntnerthor Theater, where the Ninth Symphony was first performed

quite extraordinary. Not only is the orchestra boosted by a choir in the glorious rendering of the "Ode to Joy," with its ecstatic vision of all men as brothers, but Beethoven suddenly interrupts it with a jaunty little Turkish march accompanied by Oriental-sounding percussion instruments. Through his music, Beethoven was offering the Viennese the chance to extend the hand of friendship to all nations, including their traditional enemies, the Turks. (And since the historic destruction of the Berlin Wall in 1989, this great choral finale has fittingly become the moving symbol of reconciliation between Eastern and Western Europe.)

"Ode to Joy" from the Ninth Symphony

Beethoven in his study

During the last three years of his life, Beethoven became more and more withdrawn, going out only for walks by himself, or for a drink or a meal at the local tavern. He still enjoyed his food, especially fish, macaroni cheese, cold turkey in jelly and French liver pâté, and he was particularly fond of coffee. But his temper grew steadily worse, and his closest friends had to put up with his rudeness and outbursts of rage. Once, when a waiter at his favorite restaurant brought him the wrong dish by mistake, he flung it at the unfortunate fellow's head. "The neglect of his person gives him a somewhat wild appearance," wrote an English visitor. "His features are strong and prominent: his eye is full of rude energy; his hair, which neither comb nor scissors seem to have visited for years, overshadows his broad brow in a quantity and confusion to which only the snakes round a Gorgon's head offer a parallel. Except when he is among his chosen friends, kindliness and affability are not his characteristics. The total loss of his hearing has deprived him of all the pleasures which society can give, and has perhaps soured his temper."

Beethoven out walking, sketched by J. P. Lyser

43

As he withdrew from public life, Beethoven now turned from big orchestral works – no longer popular with the public – to the intimate world of chamber music. His last pieces are all string quartets – perhaps the most demanding type of composition. He had not written any for fourteen years. But in 1822 a new patron, the Russian Prince Nikolay Golitsin, asked him for three quartets. Beethoven finished the first one, in E flat, at the end of 1824, but it was not well received by the public. The second, in A minor, was written during an illness in 1825, and the slow movement is entitled "Hymn of thanksgiving to the divinity from a convalescent." The last of the three, Op. 130 in B flat, was a huge piece in six movements, the last of which is the "Grosse Fuge" (grand fugue).

All Beethoven's later quartets were (and still are) immensely difficult, both for the players and the audience. The players couldn't cope with the Grand Fugue, and Beethoven's publisher persuaded him to write another finale and publish the fugue separately.

The last years of Beethoven's life were made even more miserable by his nephew Karl's behavior. Karl's mother

Karl van Beethoven
(1806–1858)

44

never gave up the fight for her child; and the willful boy ran away from home several times, and started seeing his mother secretly. During his teenage years poor Karl must have found life with his suspicious and grumpy uncle very difficult. Matters came to a head in 1826 when Beethoven wanted Karl to go to university, while he wanted to go into the army. Karl tried – unsuccessfully – to shoot himself. He told the police that Beethoven had "tormented" him: "I got worse because my uncle wanted me to be better." (Karl did eventually join the army. He died in 1858, and his own grandson, Karl – the last of the Beethovens – died in Vienna in 1917).

But his nephew's suicide attempt took a terrible toll on Beethoven's own health. He spent the autumn of 1826 in the country with his brother Johann, where he wrote two more string quartets. When he returned to Vienna in December he was already very ill, suffering from swollen feet (dropsy), and jaundice caused by a diseased liver. All the doctors could do to ease his pain was to drain off the fluid from his swollen

Beethoven on his deathbed, by Joseph Danhauser

stomach. Hearing of his condition, the Philharmonic Society of London sent him $160, and his publisher sent a case of fine Rhenish wine. His sufferings lasted four months. On a bitterly cold day near the end of March 1827, Beethoven turned to his companions. "Applaud, my friends," he said in Latin. "The comedy is finished." All the next day he lay in a coma. At about six o'clock in the evening, a violent snowstorm began, accompanied by thunder. At the first bolt of lightning, Beethoven opened his eyes, raised his right hand in a defiant gesture – and fell back dead.

His will left everything to Karl; as well as bank shares of 7441 florins (over $25,000 now) and payments due from patrons, he left a considerable wardrobe of clothes and some furniture as well as his books and manuscripts.

Beethoven's will

Mozart's funeral service had been attended by a handful of mourners, and no one followed his body to the grave. A crowd of nearly 20,000 lined the streets to watch Beethoven's funeral procession go by. St. Stephen's Cathedral was packed out for the service, after which Beethoven was buried at the village church of Währing. The great tragic actor Heinrich Anschütz delivered a moving address written by Beethoven's friend, the Austrian national poet Franz Grillparzer. "We, the representatives of an entire nation, come to mourn the passing of the gracious mouth by which music spoke, the man who inherited and enriched the immortal fame of Handel and Bach, of Haydn and Mozart. He was an artist, and who shall stand beside him? Because he shut himself off from the world, they called him hostile and callous ... He withdrew from his fellow-men after he had given them everything, and received nothing in return. But until his death, he preserved a father's heart for mankind. Thus he was, thus he died, thus he will live to the end of time!"

Beethoven's monument in Vienna

Beethoven's funeral procession

Glossary of Musical Terms

Minuet A courtly, graceful dance, much used for short piano pieces, or as one section (movement) of a larger orchestral piece.

Scherzo "Joke." A quick piece enclosing a slower section, which replaced the minuet as a movement in many of Beethoven's symphonies.

Sonata A piece for one or two instruments (such as piano alone, or violin with piano) in up to four movements.

Symphony A large-scale orchestral piece, usually in four separate movements (although Beethoven's 6th Symphony has five). The first and last were usually quick; the second slow, and the third was often a minuet or a scherzo (see above). Sometimes the slow movement came third.

Concerto A piece for solo instrument and orchestra often in three movements (fast, slow, fast), intended to show off the soloist's technique. The most common concertos were for piano or violin.

Chamber Music Pieces for a small but varied group of instruments, each playing an individual part.

Trio A piece of chamber music for three instruments (a piano trio consisted of piano, violin and cello).

Quartet A piece of chamber music for four instruments (a string quartet consisted of two violins, viola and cello).

Quintet A piece of chamber music for five instruments.

Sextet A piece of chamber music for six instruments.

Septet A piece of chamber music for seven instruments.

Octet A piece of chamber music for eight instruments.

Variations A form used for piano pieces, or for movements of orchestral works, in which a simple tune is treated in a series of different ways.

Opera A drama set to music, usually in several acts. *Fidelio* was sung in German.

Mass A musical setting of the Catholic service, in Latin, for church use.

List of Works

These are Beethoven's most important works in the following categories:

Symphonies
Nine: No. 1 in C (1800), No. 2 in D (1801–2), No. 3 in E♭ "Eroica" (1803), No. 4 in B♭ (1806), No. 5 in C minor (1807–8), No. 6 "Pastoral" (1808), No. 7 in A (1811–12), No. 8 in F (1812), No. 9 in D minor "Choral" (1822–4).

Orchestral
Six overtures, including *Coriolan* (1807), three *Leonora* overtures (1805–6); Ballet music for *Prometheus*; incidental music for *Egmont*, *The Ruins of Athens*, *King Stephen*; Wellington's Victory – "Battle Symphony" (1813), two romances for violin and orchestra, Choral Fantasia for piano, chorus and orchestra.

Concertos
Five for piano including No. 5 the "Emperor," one for violin, Triple Concerto for piano, violin and cello.

Chamber Music
Two string quintets, sixteen string quartets, four string trios, Octet for wind instruments, Septet for strings and wind, two Sextets for wind, one piano quintet, three piano quartets, nine piano trios.

Sonatas and Variations
Five cello sonatas, ten violin sonatas, including "Kreutzer Sonata," three sets of variations for cello and piano, one set of variations (on "se vuol ballare" from *Figaro*) for violin and piano.

Piano
Thirty-two piano sonatas, including "Pathétique," "Moonlight," "Tempest," "Waldstein," "Appassionata," "Farewell," "Hammerklavier," twenty sets of variations, including "Eroica," "God save the King," "Rule Britannia," "Diabelli," twenty-four shorter pieces, twenty-seven bagatelles.

Opera
Fidelio (1804–5).

Vocal Music
Oratorio – *Christ on the Mount of Olives* (1803), Mass in C (1807), Mass in D "Missa solemnis" (1823), eight cantatas, ninety songs, sixty canons etc., fifty folk-song settings.

VIKING
Published by the Penguin Group
Viking Penguin, a division of Penguin Books USA Inc., 375 Hudson Street, New York, New York 10014, U.S.A.
Penguin Books Ltd, 27 Wrights Lane, London W8 5TZ, England
Penguin Books Australia Ltd, Ringwood, Victoria, Australia
Penguin Books Canada Ltd, 2801 John Street, Markham, Ontario, Canada L3R 1B4
Penguin Books (N.Z.) Ltd, 182–190 Wairau Road, Auckland 10, New Zealand

Penguin Books Ltd, Registered Offices: Harmondsworth, Middlesex, England

First published in Great Britain by Faber & Faber Ltd in association with Faber Music Ltd, 1990

First American edition published in 1991
10 9 8 7 6 5 4 3 2

ISBN 0-670-83678-8
CIP data available upon request

Printed in Spain by Mateu Cromo, Madrid